TAURUS

TAURUS
April 20–May 20

NAME

SUN SIGN

MOON SIGN

RISING SIGN

Crystal Astrology for Modern Life

SANDY SITRON

CONTENTS

CRYSTALS, ASTROLOGY AND YOU

UNDERSTANDING TAURUS

TAURUS THROUGHOUT THE YEAR

LUNAR ENERGY AND MERCURY IN MOTION

CRYSTALS, ASTROLOGY AND YOU

THE STONES,
THE SIGNS AND YOU

The stars above you and the stones beneath your feet are part of the fabric of your world. Astrology offers a cosmic perspective. Crystals radiate with the healing energy of the Earth. Together, they serve as guides in your life, engaged in a vibrational conversation that can help you reflect on, and tune into, who you are. Birthstones and other crystals can be used to highlight and harness the energy of your astrological birth chart.

As above, so below – harness the power of crystals and the cosmos to create a deeper connection with yourself for a confident, empowered, high-vibe life.

Astrology is the ancient study of the changing positions and alternating energy of the celestial bodies and how this relates to our lives on Earth. The unique cosmic environment that you synced up with at the moment of your first breath provides awareness of – and offers a way to interpret – your personality traits, core strengths, growth areas, emotional style and so much more. When you better understand your vibrational self, it's easier to make informed choices about the big and small things in your life. Your conscious perspective is uplifted. Your mind is opened and activated.

Crystals, or 'stones', vibrate with the breath of the Earth. They act on an energetic level, sending vibrations out into the world. They are natural amplifiers of positive energy and bring discordant energies into balance. Each crystal has its own energy blueprint, which is why different types of stones may influence the human energy field in different ways. Pairing the insight that you gain from astrology with the healing power of crystals can help you navigate certain life areas and facilitate personal transformation and spiritual growth throughout the astrological year.

Crystals and the constellations call to us. In this book you'll receive a bespoke selection of crystals to help you amplify or balance the unique energies of your sign. You'll gain insight into your life, activate your highest potential and learn to live harmoniously with the energy that surrounds you.

When gazing at the night sky, when you hold a crystal in your hand, feel inspired to slow down, be present in the moment and get ready to embark on a meaningful journey of self-discovery.

YOUR UNIQUE RECOMMENDATIONS

We all accept that different things work for different people. Advice that's a perfect fit for one person might fall flat for someone else. Regardless of where Taurus sits in your personal astrology, this book will help you understand your Taurus nature and give you specific crystal recommendations for your sign and each astrological season. You can use these bespoke Taurus crystals to build confidence, spark creativity, feel more present, harmonize relationships, attract love, embrace your emotions, cultivate friendships, create abundance, optimize your health and wellness, amplify your natural gifts and find balance.

YOUR ASTRO-CRYSTAL JOURNEY

Once you understand how the two energetic studies of crystals and astrology relate to your life, you'll be ready to take a deep dive into your Taurus energy and learn to use crystals to leverage the strengths of your Taurus gifts, whether Taurus is your Sun, Moon or Rising sign, or elsewhere in your unique astrology. You'll also discover your unique Taurus crystal recommendations for love, friendship, money, work and health to help you connect to your true potential and reach your dreams and goals.

As each astrological season holds a different kind of energy, this book will take you through the year and show you how crystals can help you channel your unique Taurus energy under each sign. In this way, you will learn to navigate through the seasons with ease and to harmonize with the cycles of nature. You will discover how crystals can help you embrace the ebb and flow of the 29-day Moon cycle, enable you to sail through Mercury Retrograde and even plan your week.

This book is part of a series that unites each of the twelve zodiac signs with recommended crystals. When you are ready to go deeper on your astro-crystal journey, you may choose to purchase the companion books in the series that correspond to the other prominent signs in your birth chart.

THE
STONES

Dazzling gemstones are typically formed deep under the Earth's surface, stimulated by the combination of mineral-rich water, heat and pressure. Subterranean 'gardens' nurture the formation of billions of atoms into highly ordered, three-dimensional repeating patterns to create unique crystals, each one holding a vibrational record of earthly, physical reality.

Across the world and over millennia, people have been fascinated by crystals. Lucent jewels have captured the imagination for over 30,000 years. In the Democratic Republic of the Congo, small tools decorated with Quartz have been found that date back to 33,000 BCE. The Ancient Sumerians of Mesopotamia (present-day Iraq) used crystals for rituals and magic in the fourth century BCE. Humankind has used crystals for decoration, status, currency, religion, healing, magic-making and, in more recent times, modern technology. Early radios used crystals as electrical and tuning components. Today's computers, LCD screens and some batteries rely on crystal technology.

Good Vibrations People across different cultures and generations have turned to crystals as guides or helpers because it seems that, whatever facet of earthly experience you are struggling with, there is a crystal frequency that can help you move forwards on your path. Crystals may help bring calm and heal stress, empower you when you need support or confidence, or provide focus and clarity when you're struggling with an important decision. Crystals are thought to absorb the energy that you are trying to release and release the energy you are trying to absorb.

For example, if you are feeling dull and listless, Carnelian may share with you a vibration of high energy and drive. If you are overheated or stressed, Rose Quartz may help you soften and relax. Choosing the right crystal that resonates with, or reacts to, your energy can shift your mood or your mindset.

CHOOSING YOUR CRYSTALS

In Part Two of this book, you will be guided to a selection of crystals that are energetically aligned with your unique astrology. If you are adding these stones to your collection, it's important to choose responsibly.

Sustainability and Ethics   How did the crystal that you have in your hand make its way to you? The answer to this question is incredibly important to the well-being of humanity and the Earth.

The crystal industry is shrouded in mystery and plagued by bad practices. When you purchase a crystal, make sure to find gems that have a traceable, and short, journey from the mine to your hand. It's important to know if the mine that the crystal came from uses ethical, safe and sustainable practices. Discover if the lapidary, where the crystal was cut and polished, is a safe place that pays a living wage to the people who work there. The easiest way to do this is to mindfully source your crystals from sellers who have done the legwork. You vote with your financial choices. Make sure that you are contributing to better health and safety for all.

More information about sustainable and ethical practices and purveyors can be found on my website www.sandysitron.com/crystals.

Size, Finish and Price   When harnessing the power of a crystal for personal use, the size of the stone doesn't matter. If you are holding a crystal or carrying it close to your body, its vibration is in your energy field and will have an effect whatever its size.

A raw stone is a stone that is untreated. These are just as effective to use in healing practices as a crystal that has been tumbled or polished. So when you are choosing a crystal, choose one that appeals to you, no matter the size or finish.

The stones selected in this book can be sourced at an affordable price. Although some of the stones mentioned may sound ultra-luxurious and expensive, these crystals are available at a range of values.

YOUR CRYSTAL TOOLKIT

In the next section, you'll find crystal recommendations for your specific sign. First, here are a few indispensable crystals to round out your toolkit. These selections are a wonderful support for anyone at any time.

Smoky Quartz Getting grounded is the basis of spiritual work. So many factors in everyday life pull us out of ourselves. Spending too much time on your phone, not enough time in nature or eating too much sugar are common culprits, but the list goes on. If you want to nail your next meeting at work, remember where your keys are, or get on top of that to-do list, you need to get grounded. Feeling grounded also allows you to be present in your relationships and tuned in to your physical needs. This is where Smoky Quartz can help. This crystal keeps you centred, and emotionally clear. It may help you take a more practical view of a situation. On a more mystical level, Smoky Quartz has the effect of protecting you from energetic drains on your system. It is an excellent protection stone and just holding it can help you feel steady.

Selenite Just as you bathe your body regularly, it makes sense to regularly cleanse your energy system too. Energetic cleansing can help you balance your emotions and clear your mind. Cleanse your energy after work, socializing or spending time in a crowd. Or employ Selenite to help you get rid of emotional residue after a tough conversation. Energy cleansing is also recommended when you are going through any kind of transition – a break-up, a move or some other important milestone. Use Selenite with the intention of purifying your energy field and cleansing yourself of anything that is dragging you down. Imagine that it shines a ray of light through your entire body, clearing and cleansing.

Smoky Quartz Ritual	Selenite Ritual
Perform the grounding practice on page 26 while holding Smoky Quartz to anchor you.	Selenite can also be used to cleanse the energy of your other stones. Place a Selenite stone next to your crystals overnight.

SOOTHING
RELAXATION

Rose Quartz   We all know what it's like to get stressed out and frazzled. Sometimes the nervous system is overloaded and it's hard to calm down. When that happens, you need a soothing crystal ally that can help you relax. If you are having trouble sleeping, are feeling on edge, or are working through some challenging emotions, it's time to soften with Rose Quartz. This dreamy pink stone is known for its inherent ability to calm and reassure. It soothes you while strengthening your capacity for empathy and compassion. If you're feeling down, lonely or heartbroken, let this crystalline stress-reliever support you.

FINDING
YOUR DIRECTION

Clear Quartz   Clear quartz is a true all-purpose stone. When you actively set an intention with Clear Quartz, the stone will magnify that intention. When your world is changing around you and you need to forge ahead in a new direction, Clear Quartz will get you there. Clear Quartz can help you clarify, strategize and set your aspirations for your life. Once programmed with your wishes and desires, this powerful amplifier will hold the vibration of your intentions and help you visualize and realize your future.

Rose Quartz Ritual	Clear Quartz Ritual
Infuse a tumbled Rose Quartz stone in your next cup of tea or glass of water for a mindful moment with a soothing elixir.	Write an affirmation that inspires you. Say your affirmation aloud while holding Clear Quartz.

Amethyst Your intuition is your natural guidance system. It's that gut feeling you have when something feels wrong, or when something feels just right. Intuition shows up in different ways for everyone but it's like a muscle that can be strengthened. If you have questions about your life and you want to tune into the answers, Amethyst is at your service. In those moments, practice asking and listening and let this violet stone help open up your mind's eye. Amethyst is also a fantastic friend when you need help saying the right thing in your next important conversation, meeting or presentation. Or if you are looking for a sparkling boost to your creativity, open the channels of inspiration with Amethyst by your side.

	Amethyst Ritual	

The next time you have a question about your life or path, lie down and place an Amethyst stone on your forehead or near the crown of your head. Meditate and make space for the answer to come through.

THE SIGNS

ASTROLOGY AND YOU

You are a unique being, made up of a solar system of characteristics that define your identity. Astrology illuminates your personality and your path. It describes how you think, learn, love, act and much more. Astrology can also be used to understand the energy of the moment.

Astrology has been contributed to by cultures throughout the world over thousands of years. The astrology used in this book is drawn from contemporary Western astrology. Like all things in the universe, the movements of the planets through the zodiac create a vibration. At the moment of your first breath, this energy is mirrored within you.

Your astrology is much more complex than just your star sign. The movements of the planets under the zodiac, in the exact place, at the exact moment you were born form your birth chart, a personalized map of the sky from your unique vantage point on Earth when you took your first breath. As well as showing you where the Sun lands in your chart, denoting your star sign, it also shows under which signs the Moon and other planets fall – this is the key to understanding your personal energetic code.

In order to discover your unique astrological make-up first you need to map your birth chart.

SUN, MOON AND RISING SIGN

When someone asks, 'What's your sign?' they are actually referring to your Sun sign, but it's worth learning your Moon and Rising signs too. These three symbols are a good place to begin your astrological journey as they represent the basic outline of who you are – like a simple sketch that captures your likeness in just a few brushstrokes. Together these three symbols make up your inner and outer self.

Casting Your Birth Chart Go to www.sandysitron.com/crystals and enter your birth data in the 'Create Your Birth Chart' tool. You'll then receive your birth chart, also called your natal chart, that shows the signs that the planets were in when you were born, and where they were located in the sky.

SUN
SIGN

- The Sun is a constant bright light, it symbolizes your ego, the part of you that you consciously identify with. It's how you tend to think of yourself.

- The Sun is the gravitational centre of the solar system, it represents your core self and describes your fundamental character and values.

- The Sun is the energy source that creates life on our planet, it signifies how you channel your energy.

MOON
SIGN

The Moon is most visible at night, it symbolizes the part of you that is hard to see – your subconscious self.

The Moon changes shape through the lunar month. It represents your ever-changing emotions and how you respond subconsciously to your feelings.

The Moon is a satellite that circles the Earth, it describes how you turn inwards to protect, nurture and soothe yourself.

RISING
SIGN

- The Rising sign, also known as your Ascendant, is the constellation of the zodiac that was rising on the eastern horizon at the precise moment of your birth.

- The Rising sign shines new light into the world. It symbolizes how the rays of your personality beam out ahead as you walk down the street, meet new people, or interact on social media. It represents your vibe or your 'brand'. It epitomizes how other people see you.

- As you explore the following pages, you'll learn how to balance and enhance your unique energy using supportive crystals.

PLANETS

SUN
☉

MOON
☽

MERCURY
☿

VENUS
♀

MARS
♂

JUPITER
♃

SATURN
♄

URANUS
♅

NEPTUNE
♆

PLUTO
♇

DEC 22–JAN 19

JAN 20–FEB 18

FEB 19–MAR 20

MAR 21–APR 19

APR 20–MAY 20

MAY 21–JUN 21

CAPRICORN

AQUARIUS

PISCES

ARIES

TAURUS

GEMINI

AMETHYST

AQUAMARINE

JASPER

EMERALD

AGATE

DATES ARE APPROXIMATE AS THE DATES OF THE
SIGNS VARY BY ABOUT A DAY FROM YEAR TO YEAR.

ELEMENTS

FIRE
△

EARTH
▽

AIR
△

WATER
▽

MODALITY

CARDINAL
∧

FIXED
□

MUTABLE
◠

NOV 22–DEC 21

OCT 24–NOV 21

SEP 23–OCT 23

AUG 23–SEP 22

JUL 23–AUG 22

JUN 22–JUL 22

SAGITTARIUS

SCORPIO

TOPAZ

OPAL

LIBRA

SAPPHIRE

VIRGO

CARNELIAN

LEO

CANCER

TOOLS FOR
YOUR JOURNEY

As you go forwards on your astro-crystal journey, two
key tools can help you gain insight and create positive
change – intuition and intention. Intuition helps you know
what you want and intention helps you make it happen.

LETTING YOUR
INTUITION GUIDE YOU

Everyone is intuitive, your intuition or 'inner knowing' is your built-in guidance system. Use the following prompts to strengthen your inner voice.

How to Connect with Your Intuition

Slow down   Take a few deep breaths and close your eyes. The more you can slow down in your life (even for just five minutes) the louder your intuitive voice grows.

Pose a question   What do you want to know? Ask yourself. Say it aloud or ponder it silently. Or choose to write it down, sketch it or even dance it out. However you pose the question, make sure it is clear. If you aren't sure what to ask, try, 'what do I need to know that I don't yet know?'

Listen for the answer   You might hear words or notice a sensation in your body. You might write down your question in a notebook then flip the page and write down the answer. You might have an emotional response or feel compelled to move in a certain way. Pay attention.

Practice   The more you practice asking and listening, the more you get to understand your unique intuitive voice. Just as weightlifting tones your physical body, practicing these steps improves your intuitive muscle, so stick with it!

INTENTION
SETTING

In your meditations and rituals, you can program your crystals with the intentions or affirmations that will help you meet your goals.
An intention is a new thought that you would like to think. Our subconscious minds save energy by putting certain thoughts and habits on repeat. This survival skill has benefits, such as giving us more energy and space for other things, but it also has its downsides, such as getting us stuck in a negative pattern. One way to break in a new way of thinking is to intentionally repeat a new thought. Here is how to 'affirm' your new way of thinking into being!

Define what it is you would like to change.
Where are you feeling stuck? What is the pattern
that is bugging you? For example, 'I am stuck
because I have these exciting ideas for new
projects, but I never finish what I start.'

- <u>Decide what you want</u>
  For instance, 'It would be great
  if I finished my projects.'

- <u>Make it an 'I' statement</u>
  Such as, 'I finish my projects.'

- <u>Make it affirmative</u>
  Make sure your affirmation is
  positively stated. Say what you want,
  not what you don't want. So 'I finish
  my projects' not 'I no longer leave
  my projects unfinished'.

- <u>Make it in the here and now</u>
  Write your affirmation in the present
  tense: 'I finish my projects' rather
  than 'I will finish my projects'.

- <u>Describe the feeling</u>
  Include some positive descriptors,
  so that you can easily visualize
  how great it feels to realize your
  affirmation: 'I finish my projects
  and I feel so satisfied.'

- <u>Evaluate</u> Does the affirmation you
  wrote give you a positive feeling?
  If so, wonderful! You have your
  affirmation. If not, refine it. You may
  need a 'stepping stone' to make your
  affirmation more believable. For
  example, if you have a complicated
  track record with finishing what you
  begin, your subconscious mind may
  need more help believing 'I finish
  my projects and I feel so satisfied'.
  In that case try, 'I believe in the
  possibility that I finish my projects
  and feel satisfied', or 'I'm learning to
  finish my projects with satisfaction
  and ease'. With time and practice
  you'll find that you no longer need
  the stepping stone and you can
  update your affirmation to 'I easily
  finish my projects and I'm filled
  with satisfaction!'

WAYS TO
WORK WITH
CRYSTALS

Crystals are a powerful force as they are but,
in order to optimize their benefits, discover how
to care for and recharge them with regular
cleansing, and learn how to activate them using
the intentions you've developed.

CLEANSE YOUR CRYSTALS

Everything on Earth must go through a
process of decay and renewal. Cleansing your
crystals can help them reset with a clear energetic
frequency. When you cleanse a crystal, imagine
that you are clearing it of any energy that it may
have picked up from yourself, other people
and the environment.

How to Cleanse Your Crystals

Make sure to research your stone to discover if the method you are considering is safe for both you and the crystal. For example, some crystals may dissolve in water or fade in sunlight. Some stones contain trace minerals that may be physically harmful when released into water.

Light: Place your crystal in sunlight or moonlight for an hour.
Salt: Immerse your crystal in salt for about five minutes.
Sound: Chant or use an instrument such as singing bowls, chimes or tuning forks.
Water: Wash your crystal under running water, from a natural water source or a tap, for a few minutes.
Visualization: Imagine crystalline light or archangels surrounding your crystal with the intention of cleansing.
Selenite: Place selenite next to your crystal and leave in place overnight.
Earth: Bury your crystal underground for about a day.

When to cleanse your crystals

It's a good idea to cleanse your crystal when you first get it and about once a month after that. Cleanse more often if you use your crystals regularly.

GROUND
YOURSELF

Before you do any kind of energy work, it's important to get grounded. When a ship puts down its anchor in a quiet harbour, it's protected from being pulled by strong waves back into the sea. As you engage in energy work with crystals, you may drift and dream far afield. It protects you to have an anchor that keeps you connected to the Earth.

How to Get
Grounded

· To begin, set yourself up in a quiet and comfortable space, either seated or lying down. Close your eyes. Imagine that your torso is like a tree trunk with roots growing down through your feet.

· Breathe comfortably and deeply as you imagine your roots flowing down through the ground and all the way to the Earth's core.

· Visualize a healing light moving up through your roots into your body. Imagine this healing light circulating through your body and carrying any tension or stress away and out, and back down into the Earth.

· Continue to imagine the energy flow – grounding energy coming up through your roots, tension and stress flowing back down to the Earth.

· When you feel relaxed and grounded, give thanks to the Earth before you open your eyes.

ACTIVATE YOUR CRYSTALS

Now that your crystal is cleansed and you are grounded, you can 'program' your crystal with the intention you've developed. Programming your crystal is one way to activate it so that its vibrations are attuned to your desires and goals. It's as simple as telling your crystal what you intend to create or achieve.

How to Program Your Intention

To amplify your crystal's power, focus your thoughts on your intention and train that energy towards your crystal.

- Make sure you have a clear intention or affirmation.

- Set a timer for ten minutes.

- Sit comfortably either in a chair or on the floor.

- Hold your crystal or place it on your body. You could also place it on the floor or on a table in front of you.

- On each inhale, repeat your intention out loud or in your mind.

- On each exhale bring your attention to your crystal.

- When you notice your attention wandering, bring your awareness back to the crystal and your breath.

- Repeat until your timer sounds.

TAURUS

DATES: APRIL 20–MAY 20 **ELEMENT:** EARTH
MODALITY: FIXED **PLANET:** VENUS **SYMBOL:** BULL
CRYSTAL: EMERALD

YOUR SIGN, EXPLAINED

Steady, lush, sensual Taurus. You are like a master gardener, cultivating beauty and abundance that sustains life and dazzles the senses. The Taurus mantra is 'I build'– you plan, work hard, and enjoy the benefits. The bounty you create is so beautiful to behold that through your sustained effort you remind everyone that life is good and precious. For as much as you push forwards with determination, you also know how to lean back and enjoy the sensual and physical experience of life on Earth. You are diligent, practical, creative and artistic.

Taurus is in it for the long haul – slow and steady wins the race. You stick with the plan even when it's difficult. Your Taurus energy shines when you are driven and dedicated.

A deep, embodied and gracious being, you don't shy away from luxury and extra flourishes. In fact, your aspirations for a life enriched with beauty and pleasure are what make all of your effort and hard work feel worth it.

Your earthy sign not only symbolizes practical needs such as food, water, shelter, money and security, but takes things one step further and signifies the sensual opportunities of life on Earth. Taurus enjoys tantalizing tastes and scents, velvety touches, celestial sounds and glorious visions.

Solid, unhurried, gentle and enduring, you achieve because you have the ability to persevere. You push through obstacles with stubborn resilience. With strength and grace, you create worth and value in the world around you and in yourself.

TAURUS IS AN EARTH SIGN

Earth is the physical, the practical, the sensible and sensual. It's the ground beneath your feet. You focus on the basic necessities of life – food, water and shelter. And you take it one step further by appreciating beauty and pleasure as well.

TAURUS IS A PERSONAL SIGN

As the first of the three Earth signs, Taurus is a Personal sign. Personal signs are playful and encourage you to explore without regard to outside factors such as other people, or the world around you. Taurus emphasizes how you experience the world through your physical body and your five senses – touch, taste, smell, sight and sound.

TAURUS IS A FIXED SIGN

The Fixed signs dig in and hold on. This energy keeps projects going, even when times are tough. The steady attitude of the Fixed signs works to build and maintain. You like to finish what you start.

TAURUS IS RULED BY THE PLANET VENUS

Venus is the soft and gentle goddess of love, relationships, abundance and beauty. This planet represents the part of you that receives and allows. Venus brings receptivity, gentleness, softness and grace to the sign of Taurus.

THE BULL IS THE SYMBOL FOR TAURUS

This animal symbolizes virility, fertility, abundance and strength. Taurus is persistent and steadfast like the Bull.

EMERALD IS A KEY CRYSTAL BIRTHSTONE FOR TAURUS

Emerald helps you connect with your heart, your courage and your inner wisdom. This gentle and inspiring stone will help you love yourself fully so that you feel whole. With potent Emerald by your side, the courage to take risks and the motivation to follow through on your goals is amplified.

TAURUS
TRAITS

———————

Your key traits show how you shine.
These are the special characteristics
that make you unique.

———————

Grounded   You are steady, practical and grounded. While others may be motivated by fantasies or ideals, you tend to ensure that your basic needs are met and that you are investing in your future.

Sensual   Although you are sensible, you are also sensual. You have excellent taste, and you surround yourself with beauty and luxury – soft fabrics, gentle sights and sounds, delicious foods. You prioritize beauty and pleasure.

Persistent   You're in it for the long game. You know that long-term rewards require consistent effort.

Patient   You are unhurried and patient. You let others take their time too.

Prudent   You know the value of things. This can help you make sensible financial choices.

Physical   You are strongly aware of your sense of touch, and you love to engage in physical activities. Massage is very healing for you.

Gentle   Mellow, pleasant and sweet-tempered, you have an air of calm and grace.

Resilient   Even under stress you endure.

Artistic   You are creative and you have a natural sense of balance and beauty.

———————

Your natural gifts offer both strengths and
challenges. The same traits that make you
special may also require balance at times.

———————

Laid-back vs Lazy   You can be very
relaxed and unhurried. When your
motivation lags, you may start to
become a bit lazy.

Steady vs Stubborn   When you make
a plan or commitment, you work slowly
and consistently towards your goals.
However, there are times when you
need to change course. Let go when
you need to.

Satisfaction vs Self-Indulgence
Comfort and satisfaction are important
to you. At times, your desire to feel good
can turn into self-indulgence.

Material vs Materialistic
The material side of life is very
important to you – money, beauty
and luxury. Sometimes, these earthly
priorities may distort into an overly
materialistic attitude.

Productive vs Possessive   Because
of your strong work ethic, you attain
the things you want and need. But
you may find that it's hard to let go
or share. You have a strong sense of
ownership that can sometimes morph
into possessiveness.

Loyal vs Limited   When someone
meets your high standards, you are a
loyal friend for life. But until others
prove themselves, you keep your social
circle limited.

Compatibility is a complex feature of astrology because you are more than just your Sun sign. And other people are multi-faceted too.

Friends

You settle into a comfortable routine with **Cancer**. Together, you feel safe and loved. The Crab makes it easy for you to be yourself and you remind **Cancer** to be more practical.

With productivity pal **Virgo** on your team, you'll feel awakened to new possibilities.

You supply the raw materials and **Capricorn** helps you build a skyscraper. Together, you are limitless.

Turn to **Pisces** when you need to escape into a world of beauty, enchantment and wonder. You bring reality and **Pisces** brings imagination. Together, you make magic on earth.

Foes

Aries can be so over the top that you might find yourself needing to slip away to rest and recuperate in the predictable safety of your cosy abode.

Gemini's rapid-fire thought process can leave you overstimulated. You might start craving a chance to hear yourself think.

Sagittarius has big ideas and fervent opinions. Sometimes the combination can cause you to doubt yourself and your own inner wisdom.

While **Aquarius** concocts something new and unusual, you might yearn to stick to the recipe that you know and love. Change is not always good.

CANCER	VIRGO	ARIES	GEMINI
CAPRICORN	PISCES	SAGITTARIUS	AQUARIUS

TAURUS
SUN

If you were born April 20–May 20, Taurus is your Sun sign (check your birth chart for an exact calculation). Your Sun sign describes your basic energy.

Just as the Sun is the centre of the solar system, your Sun sign (also called your zodiac sign or star sign) symbolizes the core of your being. As a Taurus Sun, you deeply value security, beauty and growth. Integrity, worth and value are also very important to you. These concepts make you feel strong and grounded. You are constantly developing your personal integrity as well as your sense of self-worth.

Because you are persistent and loyal, you develop deep roots. As you grow, you may resist uprooting yourself to embrace new ways of being. At these times you can benefit from more flexibility and openness to change.

Because your Sun sign fuels your confidence and enlivens your sense of self, there are two recommended crystals for Taurus Sun. The Amplifying crystal will help you expand upon your gifts and the Balancing crystal will help you integrate your growth areas.

37

TAURUS SUN
AMPLIFYING CRYSTAL

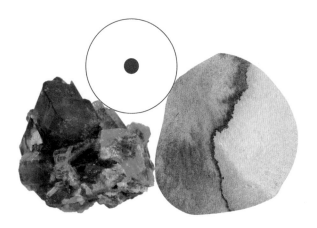

SELF-WORTH, LOVE,
HEART-OPENING

Emerald Through the gateway of the heart, Emerald helps you feel valuable, lovable and worthy. Emerald is a glimmering green Beryl that is thought to help you connect to your heart centre. Emerald supercharges your loving nature, helping you first extend love to yourself, then to others. When you radiate an energy of love, you contribute to the peace and harmony in the world.

If you need a reason to love yourself more, the simple fact that you are alive is enough. Emerald helps you emotionally connect with this truth – you don't have to do anything or be anything. You are enough as you are.

When you feel pumped up with love and self-worth, it's easier to be courageous. So, when you yearn to feel imbued with confidence or bravery, begin with your heart. Let Emerald help you boost yourself so that you can feel gentle, peaceful, loving and bold. Your heart-centered actions will take you far.

TAURUS SUN
BALANCING CRYSTAL

**CLEARING, ATTUNEMENT,
INTUITION**

Selenite   Selenite is a luminous crystal that is often transparent but can be found in a range of colours and opacities. As your Taurus nature endeavours to cultivate deep roots, you may sometimes find it hard to pivot or change. Selenite can help balance these tendencies as it brings in a wave of clearing and cleansing energies that can awaken fresh insights and open up a higher perspective. By opening your mind to your true self, Selenite prompts you to overcome stagnation and allows you to find new opportunities for growth and opportunity.

Selenite helps you clear out any feelings of fear and tune into your inner wisdom. It is like a gentle breeze that refreshes you and keeps things moving, so that you don't get stuck.

Turn to Selenite when you need a new perspective on an old issue, when you feel insecure or when you crave a reset.

TAURUS MOON

HEALING, AWARENESS, INNER WISDOM

In the same way that the Moon always appears to be changing shape in the sky, the Moon in your chart symbolizes the part of you that is always changing – your emotions.

Imagine that when you have an emotion come up, the Taurus part of you steps to centre stage. This happens throughout the day. It doesn't matter if the emotion is happiness, sadness, frustration or exhilaration – when emotions arise you go into full Taurus mode. Your grounded, sensible, stubborn, persistent, physical and loyal side is accentuated.

When emotions rise, you look for something steady to lean on. Usually, this security comes from something you've cultivated deep within yourself – a belief system, a strong sense of self-worth, a feeling of ownership and pride, a plan for the future.

As a Taurus Moon, you are, for the most part, incredibly calm under pressure. But like your symbol, the Bull, when you are provoked, you have a fearsome temper. Your best path to emotional self-soothing is through the beauty of the physical world. Tantalizing tastes and scents, velvety touches, celestial sounds and glorious visions envelop you and help you feel enlivened and balanced.

Your Taurus Moon crystal may help you try a new way of responding when emotions arise.

Blue Kyanite   You are a gentle soul who applies care, persistence and grace to your endeavours. Blue Kyanite can help open your psychic awareness to the impact of your life on Earth, so that you know, on a deeper level, your full value and worth in the world.

Blue Kyanite can range from pale blue-grey to deep indigo. Reach for it when you need to release your grip on an old way of reacting and negotiate a new energetic response. If you find yourself sabotaging your progress, overreacting to a change in plans, or struggling to let go, let Kyanite help you clear the old pattern, tune into your inner wisdom, and open up to a new opportunity in life or love.

TAURUS RISING

HARMONY,
PRACTICALITY, ACTION

Your Rising Sign is the sign that was on the eastern horizon when you were born. It represents the face you show to the world – your social personality. As a Taurus Rising, you radiate a glow of both beauty and strength. Your sign is a bit paradoxical, making you both dove-soft and ox-strong. When you enter a room, you bring an air of grace, polish and stabilizing practicality. Everyone around you can breathe a little easier because you radiate steadiness and charm.

Others perceive you to be pleasure-loving, epicurean and patient. You manage to get a lot done with an air of unhurried confidence. When it comes to group endeavours, you tend to be the backbone of the whole operation. You're the most valuable player, and everyone wants you on their team. When times are tough and hope is lost, you remind everyone around you of the value and purpose of the project while your enduring spirit keeps morale high.

With gracious Venus as your ruling planet, you emanate harmony. Seek out the support of a crystal that can amplify your natural air of peacefulness while also inspiring you to take practical action.

Apricot Agate   Apricot Agate bathes you in a rosy glow. With its gentle energy, Apricot Agate magnifies your serene nature. You are usually composed, but if the stress of daily life ever gets the better of you, reach for this soothing agate to restore peace and harmony.

Apricot Agate doesn't just share a calming energy. It offers a balanced mix of peace and pep, so when you want to take practical action, keep this stone by your side. For Taurus Rising, Apricot Agate offers the full package – it amplifies your natural softness and helps you take practical action towards your dreams.

OTHER TAURUS SUPPORT CRYSTALS

The following crystals are helpful for all Taurus placements – your Sun, Moon, Rising Sign and any other Taurus planet you may have in your chart. This collection of powerful Taurus crystals will give you a little extra sparkle in each of the important life areas of love, friendship, money, work and health. Harness the potential of these stones for clarity and ease in important life areas.

Everyone has different goals for romantic love. In addition, your wishes or desires can change over time. You may wish to attract or pursue love. Perhaps you are hoping to deepen your ability to love, or to open up to intimacy physically, emotionally or spiritually.

As a Taurus, you are loyal and steady in love. With your gifts of tenderness, patience and sensuality, your loving relationships flourish like a well-tended garden. Never one to rush, at times you may need a bit of prodding to take the risk of opening up. You are well served by a crystal friend that can give you the courage to put your heart on the line.

**CONFIDENCE
VITALITY
ENERGY**

Carnelian Carnelian fires up your engines and helps you put yourself out there when it comes to love and romance. This warming crystal is a great source of vitality, supporting you when you need a boost of energy. This orange stone will restore your confidence if you get burned by love, or it can bolster your courage if you need to make the first move. If you want to rekindle the spark of love, reach for Carnelian to help you break free from routine. Taurus loves to get physical, and Carnelian can amplify sexual energy, helping you sizzle and glow.

Friends offer support, fun, love and new perspectives. With Taurus prominently placed in your chart you are a steady and dependable friend. You love alone time, but somehow you are always surrounded by adoring fans. You effortlessly bring harmony and support to your friendships, and you make it look so easy that sometimes others forget to return the favour.

In friendship, you need a crystal that helps you feel supported by others and empowered in your relationships.

Chrysocolla When you reach for Chrysocolla you sync with its soothing and harmonizing energy. This green, blue or blue–green stone offers gentleness and strength, which you can bring to your friendships. As a Taurus, you count on your friends to be there for you. You are there for them in return, solid and steady as an oak tree. Chrysocolla helps you lean back and receive support from your friends without worrying or overthinking. When you have something you need to say, this crystal supports you in speaking from your heart and communicating in simple terms.

**PEACE
ABUNDANCE
LOVE**

Astrological insight can help enhance your money-making potential. Your Taurus prosperity gifts are strength, dependability, quality, persistence, practicality, simplicity, abundance and beauty. If you'd like to make more money, look to these qualities for inspiration. What feels sustainable? How does being involved with projects and products that are high-quality inspire you? How does beauty inspire you? How can you keep finances and systems simple? As a Taurus, you value security, so staying focused on your long-term financial goals eases your mind. You may find that you have a low tolerance for risk. Your sign rules wealth so devote energy to budgeting and investing.

HARMONY
PROSPERITY
STABILITY

Green Jade Taurus is the 'builder' of the zodiac. Building up wealth and security is one of the things you were born to do. Before you have your nest egg saved, or while you are experimenting with investments, it helps to create a feeling of security within yourself. Green Jade has a harmonizing energy that offers a sense of peace and stability, even when situations are uncertain. Green Jade is a classic prosperity stone, helping you trust that things will work out. This self-trust is what buffers and buoys you, so that you feel motivated to keep working and also able to relax and recharge when desired.

TAURUS × WORK

You thrive when you come up with a plan that works and you stick with it. You love to build and cultivate, and you believe in long-term gain. Your ideal working life involves projects that are solid, realistic and profitable. You need to remember that change and surprises are to be expected and that you will always have to make adjustments to a shifting environment.

You enjoy endeavours that have a real-world, tangible aspect to them. When you align your work with your values then you can really stick with it for the long term. Slow and steady wins the race when it comes to your career achievement.

Copper Copper isn't just for coins! This tawny metal is immensely useful and valuable, just like you, Taurus. Never underestimate how much others rely on you. And when you need a reminder of your worth, keep Copper close to bring you confidence. Copper is an excellent conductor of heat, and it can inject energy and drive into your working life as well. Turn to this element when you need a jolt of energy or a burst of luck. As a Taurus, you have endurance and natural strength, but copper can give you the extra dash of confidence and initiative you sometimes crave. It's like the spark of inspiration that's been there by your side all along. If you're feeling lethargic, this element will help you push through.

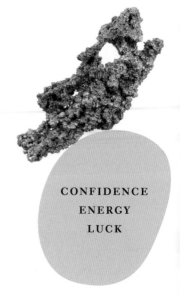

CONFIDENCE

ENERGY

LUCK

Like your symbol, the Bull, you have a robust and sturdy constitution. You are the embodiment of endurance. Your physical body is supported by consistent daily activity. Taurus loves food and the finer things of life, so investing in high-quality ingredients and allowing for small indulgences will keep you feeling balanced. As an Earth sign, your mental and emotional health is deeply intertwined with your physical body, so make sure to follow simple, healthy habits such as drinking plenty of water, walking and eating a balanced diet. Improve your general well-being by soothing your emotions and connecting with your heart. For health, seek out a crystal that helps you stay committed to your goals and make your well-being a priority.

**NURTURING
GROUNDING
HEALING**

Rhodonite   This rosy crystal is the balm you've been looking for. Let it take you on an emotional journey of healing and restoration. As you soothe your heart and fill your emotional cup with the healing energy of Rhodonite, you may find you have more energy for staying consistent with your goals. This crystal's grounding and loving energy can help you remember to take care of yourself and nurture your overall health.

TAURUS
THROUGHOUT
THE YEAR

The energies of the zodiac signs affect us throughout the year. In astrology, there is a season for everything. Feeling separated from nature's cycles and rhythms can make you feel out of step or off-kilter. It may add to stress and drain energy. Understanding and attuning to astrology's seasons might help you feel enlivened.

Take this attunement one step further by using crystals to amplify the unique energy of each moment, so that you feel fully aligned with the rhythms of nature.

The following pages take you on a journey with the sun as it passes through the twelve signs of the zodiac on its annual rotation. You will discover the key energies of each season, along with a sign-specific horoscope that aligns with the important themes of your unique chart.

CONFIDENCE AND LEADERSHIP

Aries season is the signal that begins the horse race. And they're off! This is the moment to gallop at top speed towards your goals. Put yourself out there with confidence. Make bold decisions and step in time with your intuition. This season is about saying YES to who you are and living your life with freedom. The buds are beginning to emerge and new life is beginning. Sync up with this feeling of potential and possibility.

TAURUS HOROSCOPE FOR ARIES SEASON

Turn your attention inwards, drift and dream. You may have a flood of feelings rising up during this season. The Sun is touring an introspective and sensitive zone of your chart. Focus on investigating your inner world, your emotions and your spirituality. Productivity may feel impossible – instead, let your imagination lead the charge.

Morning Practice	Evening Practice
Get your heart rate up with some fiery cardio exercise.	Cool down that inner fire with a soothing herbal tea.

CONFIDENCE

Hessonite Garnet   Developing confidence is a practice of establishing deep self-trust. Let Hessonite Garnet's activating and powerful energy help you build up your courage so that you can just go for it. Also try Green Aventurine, Orange Calcite or Malachite.

LIVING BOLDLY

Pink Aventurine   When the time is ripe for taking bold action, Pink Aventurine can help you advance into your next adventure. Reach for it when you need a boost of fun. This spirited crystal connects you with your heart centre, and acts as your best accomplice in bravery and boldness. Or choose Ruby, Tangerine Quartz or Sardonyx.

DRIVE

Fire Agate   Aries season is the vehicle in which to follow your passions and desires, which makes Fire Agate the gasoline. Whether you need to get an important project going or just tackle spring cleaning, put yourself on track to get things done by syncing up with the vibration of this fierce crystal. You could also reach for Bloodstone, Stromatolite or Cinabrite.

MONEY AND
SELF-WORTH

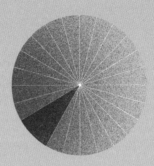

Like working in a garden and then enjoying the beauty that
you've cultivated, Taurus represents sustained effort that
leads to a productive reward. This season is the prime time
to focus on building up your sense of personal worth and
value. On one level, this process may involve nurturing your
self-esteem. On another level, this may include thinking
about security, money and finances. Taurus season is also a
time to remember the beauty of life. It reminds us that no
matter what is going on, there are simple pleasures to be had

TAURUS HOROSCOPE
FOR TAURUS SEASON

Cultivate confidence during Taurus
season. The Sun is illuminating your
zone of identity and personality. It's
time to be yourself! With boldness
and bravery, take the stage. Take risks
and, most of all, have fun. This is your
special season, so enjoy the spotlight.
Revel in the present moment and light
up every room.

Morning Practice	Evening Practice
Practice gratitude by reminding yourself of three things you're grateful for.	Do something that feels good to your body, like stretching or wearing soft clothing.

MONEY MAGIC

Green Jade   No matter where you are beginning financially, Green Jade will juice up your money situation. This abundance stone has a way of amplifying your potential. A soft and expansive prosperity stone that soothes the spirit, it will support you as you make wise financial decisions. Reach for it when you crave a feeling of security. You could also use Pyrite, Emerald or Epidote.

SELF-WORTH

Red Jasper   Red Jasper will amp up your self-appreciation quotient. Choose Red Jasper when you're feeling uncertain, if your confidence could use a boost, or if you want to feel more resilient in any way. This stone will get you in the groove of trusting your own value. Also try Carnelian, Chrysocolla or Bixbite.

ABUNDANCE

Green Apatite   If you are feeling like something in your life is lacking, such as money, time, energy, sleep, or support, for example, you might need to boost your sense of abundance. Taurus season is the perfect time to grasp hold of that feeling of nature's plentifulness. Use Green Apatite to replenish your energy and help you feel satisfied and satiated with what you have. You could also reach for Golden Tourmaline, Uvarovite Garnet or Agate.

VALUES
AND COMMUNITY

Gemini energy is like a buzzing bee that moves from flower to flower in a garden. This season is a time of mental stimulation, new ideas, learning, communicating and sharing. Use Gemini season to evaluate or challenge your mindset and values. Which attitudes are no longer serving you? What's truly important to you? Gemini season is also a time to connect with others in the community. What can you learn from others? What can you teach others? It's a fun and lively season full of new connections.

TAURUS HOROSCOPE
FOR GEMINI SEASON

Feel centred and strong. The Sun is lighting up your area of security, money and worth. What helps you feel secure? Build upon the habits and thoughts that stabilize you. This is an opportunity to deepen your sense of self-worth, through positive self-talk and confidenc building. Your mindset around money i up for review and refinement.

Morning Practice	Evening Practice
Help a new mindset emerge with a potent Gemini season intention.	Before falling asleep, envision yourself having a great time at a party surrounded by everyone you love.

CRYSTALS FOR GEMINI SEASON

MASTER YOUR MINDSET

Heliodor   Have repeating thoughts, fears or anxieties been plaguing you? Use the revitalizing energy of Gemini season and Heliodor to hit the reset button on these old thought patterns. This stone will gently help you harmonize your thoughts and adjust your mindset, helping you reconnect with your true values. Alternatively, try Blue Lace Agate, Chrome Chalcedony or Dragonstone.

CONNECTING

Agatized Coral   When you really want to feel connected, seen, heard and understood, reach for Agatized Coral. This fossilized coral nudges you to reach out to others and helps you analyse your relationships, whether with friends, lovers, family, neighbours or colleagues. It relays an upbeat feeling so that you can view your relationships with the people in your life with optimism. You may also choose Citrine, Apricot Agate or Bismuth.

COMMUNICATION

Aquamarine   Aquamarine is your crystal-clear communication companion. Communication helps us feel connected, and allows us to learn and grow. In those moments when you feel confused or foggy, this elegant stone will help you become grounded and steady. Use Aquamarine to find your voice – it will help you tune into your own true message and the truth of those around you. Alternatively, reach for Turquoise, Prairie Tanzanite or Green Chrysocolla.

HOME AND NURTURE

Come on home to Cancer season. Like Cancer's symbol, the Crab, wrap yourself in a protective shell and reflect on your life and your feelings. In Cancer season, engage in meaningful self-care, and also put your energy into nurturing others. Discover what makes you feel safe and cosy. This could be your actual home, your closest relationships or tending to the feelings and needs of your inner child.

TAURUS HOROSCOPE FOR CANCER SEASON

Let learning inspire you. It's one thing to get distracted by information; it's another to seek out knowledge that sparks new ideas. Share your wisdom with friends and neighbours. With the Sun touring your zone of communication, friends and ideas, this is an exciting season to connect with others, to learn and to grow.

Morning Practice

Let your inner child take the lead:
what do they want to do today?

Evening Practice

Sing a lullaby to soothe your
inner child before bed.

CRYSTALS FOR CANCER SEASON

NURTURING

Blue Calcite   What do you want to actively care for?
Yourself? A child? A creative project? In order to feel truly
nurturing, you need to feel inspired by love. Blue Calcite will
help you soften and open up your heart centre, so that you
feel drawn to put your compassionate and attentive energy
where it is needed most. Other nurturing crystals include
Moonstone, Blue Chalcedony and Bumblebee Jasper.

HOME ENVIRONMENT

Pink Mangano Calcite   Home is where you are safe and
protected. It's your emotional nest where you can relax. Use
Pink Mangano Calcite to create a grounded and peaceful
home environment. This stone acts as a balm that will help
you feel harmonized. Place this rosy crystal in your inner
sanctum and set the intention to soothe conflict and soften
your environment so that you can restore your energy after a
long day or week. You could also try Chiastolite, Rose Quartz
or Peach Moonstone.

FAMILY BONDS

Bornite   Family, whether chosen or blood-related, represent
some of our closest relationships. Use Bornite to foster the
strength of family relationships. This is a joyful stone that
will help you embrace the positives that come from your
family circle, while at the same time grounding you to help
you remember who you are as an individual. Also try Orange
Calcite, Indigo Gabbro or Girasol Quartz.

CREATIVITY
AND FUN

Harnessing your creativity and expressing your
true self with others, that's the key to making the most of Leo
season. It's all about playful sharing and creative shining.
Radiate your magnificent heart of gold outwards with
immediacy, freedom, spontaneity, generosity and a giant
sense of fun. During this season of wholehearted
self-expression, take a little time to remember how unique
you are. Remember what inspires you and reflect on what
you love most about yourself.

TAURUS HOROSCOPE
FOR LEO SEASON

Emotions are flowing during this time. The Sun is shining light in the area of your chart that rules home, family and tender feelings. Fill your cup by connecting with those in your inner circle and spending time at home. Tending to your emotions will free up energy so that you can be creative and have fun.

Morning Practice

Create daily.

Evening Practice

Seek out a chance to laugh every day and go to bed with a smile on your face.

INSPIRATION

Rutilated Quartz   Inspiration is the creative spark and Rutilated Quartz can help you turn that spark into a roaring bonfire. Make Leo season feel lit up with creativity. Keep Rutilated Quartz by your side when you need an inventive solution to a problem at work, when your love life could use an inspiring reboot, or when you are ready to awaken the artist within. Set your intentions and let this highly programmable stone carry the flame of your dreams. You could also use Sunstone, Golden Labradorite or Yellow Sapphire.

SELF-APPRECIATION

Thulite   Leo season is the time to shed all insecurities and put your faith in your one true self. Loving yourself dissolves insecurity and self-criticism. Thulite tunes you into the vibration of love, peace and harmony, allowing you to be present and wholly yourself. Alternatively, reach for Ruby, Larimar, or Desert Jasper.

COURAGE

Golden Apatite   To ensure your lion-heartedness knows no bounds, you need to fire up your courage. Golden Apatite bestows upon you both passion and discernment, which determine which fears are baseless. Use it when you need to take a risk at work, strike up a conversation with someone you admire or stand up for your values. Other courage-giving crystals are Carnelian, Iolite-Sunstone or Citrine.

HEALTH
AND HABITS

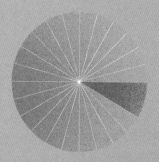

Our goals and dreams require a big-picture view,
but Virgo season reminds us that life is actually lived in the
small details. Focus on how you are living your life, your
everyday routines and rituals. On a practical level, what is
important to you? Virgo energy helps you take a closer
look at your health and habits, and how you can be
of service to others as well.

TAURUS HOROSCOPE
FOR VIRGO SEASON

Let yourself celebrate, be joyful and have
fun! The Sun is illuminating your sector
of creative self-expression and heartfelt
happiness. What do you just love to
do? It's important to ask yourself that
question periodically and make room in
your schedule for fun experiences. Be
creative and shine brightly.

Morning Practice

Drink a glass of water
first thing.

Evening Practice

Write down one task you're
going to complete tomorrow,
and stick to it.

FOCUS

Clear Quartz   Virgo season ushers in a chance to notice the
details and get focused. Use Clear Quartz to take you all the
way there. This cleansing stone helps you rivet your attention on
your commitments. When you program Clear Quartz with your
intention for focus, you'll find that it supports you, whether you
have a tight deadline or you just really need to concentrate. You
could also turn to Vanadinite, Amazonite or Tiger Iron.

HEALTH

Chevron Amethyst   A lot of factors go into maintaining
optimum health: genetics, diet, exercise, access to care, to
name just a few. Virgo season energy will encourage you
to think wisely about the preventative measures that you
can take to boost both your mental well-being and physical
health. Use Chevron Amethyst for gentle motivation that can
help you happily embrace healthier choices. Or try Girasol
Quartz, Ruby Fuchsite or Black Tourmaline.

ALTRUISM

Stromatolite   Humanity wouldn't be a successful species
without the desire to be of service to others. Virgo season plus
Stromatolite is your recommendation for kindness and selfless
action. Turn your attention to what you can do to help others,
whether that's volunteering, making a donation to a good
cause, or simply smiling and being friendly. Let Stromatolite
amplify your altruistic nature. Alternatively, reach for
Stichtite, Rhodonite or Rose Quartz.

RELATIONSHIPS AND BALANCE

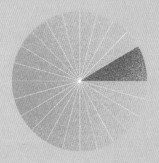

Libra season is symbolized by balanced scales. It's a chance to look at all life areas and judge the equilibrium. Are your relationships in balance? Do both people in your relationships have what they want and need? This can be a fun and harmonious time to socialize. During Libra season, balance can also be created in your environment through art, decoration and organization. The scales are the symbol for justice and Libra season brings a collective yearning to make the systems of government more fair and to expose inequalities.

TAURUS HOROSCOPE FOR LIBRA SEASON

It's time to turn your attention to the details of your life. The Sun is traversing your zone of habits, organization, health and service. Evaluate the practical parts of your life. Can you find more streamlined and effective ways of getting things done? This is a great time to create healthy habits that last.

Affirmation
BALANCE EXISTS IN ALL AREAS OF MY LIFE.

Morning Practice	**Evening Practice**
Reach out and message someone who is important to you, and tell them why.	Meditate to create mental balance.

HEALTHY BOUNDARIES

Iolite   Communicating what you want, need and desire is a great starting point to gain clarity in your relationships. Iolite can help you reflect and get to know yourself – the first step to speaking and sharing your truth with others. Once your inner base is stabilized, Iolite can help you reach out to another person, while maintaining your own healthy boundaries. This healing stone has a peaceful energy that helps you create balance between yourself and a partner. You could also use Amazonite, Purple Jade or Chiastolite.

BALANCE

Shungite   Balance is an active state, requiring constant adjustment. It comes under the jurisdiction of the intellectual, analytical sign of Libra. Keep checking in with yourself throughout Libra season to determine what needs more balance. For a crystal that will help you stay steady, reach for Shungite. Or choose Diopside, Selenite or Turquoise.

DECISIVENESS

Ametrine   Libra season is an excellent time to analyse, think things through and come up with new ideas. Keep Ametrine by your desk for productive planning sessions and for when you have big decisions to make. This balancing stone will help you keep your life on track. As an alternative, try Variscite, Fluorite or White Sapphire.

TRANSFORMATION
AND FORGIVENESS

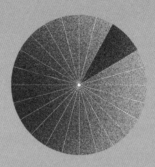

Scorpio season pulls you deeper – emotionally, physically and spiritually. This is a season of transformation, helping you to feel deeply, release old emotions and thought patterns, and get ready to move on to the next stage. By pulling back the layers and being honest with the truth of who you are, it's also an opportunity to deepen your relationships with others by letting them get to know the real you.

TAURUS HOROSCOPE
FOR SCORPIO SEASON

Decide what you want to say and what you should not say. Relationships are on your mind as the Sun is putting the spotlight on your primary partnerships. Communication is key.

The challenge to express yourself clearly is heightened. But you can rise to the occasion! Now is the moment to practice listening with empathy while also advocating for yourself.

Affirmation

I RELEASE THE PAST TO MAKE SPACE FOR NEW BEGINNINGS.

Morning Practice

Forgive yourself
for something.

Evening Practice

Forgive someone else
for something.

INTIMACY

Red Tourmaline   Scorpio season propels you to create warmth and closeness. But opening yourself up to the vulnerability of intimacy demands courage. Whether you are setting the stage for sexual intimacy or emotional intimacy, Red Tourmaline will help you feel confident enough to embrace deep connection with others. Other crystals for intimacy are Garnet, Shiva Lingam or Red Aventurine.

TRANSFORMATION

Moldavite   Transformation brings both endings and new beginnings. Moldavite will help you spiritually and emotionally adjust when change comes into your life – when a relationship has run its course, a shift is needed in the work arena or a new adventure calls your name. When the transformation you are undergoing is more subtle in texture, like saying goodbye to an old habit, Moldavite will help you align with your new reality. Or try Shungite, Moss Agate or Tugtupite.

FORGIVENESS

Dioptase   Whether you need to be kinder to yourself or let go of hurt that someone else has caused you, forgiveness doesn't happen all at once. It's a process that you set in motion. Finding forgiveness requires self-love, self-worth and understanding. Dioptase can help you practice forgiveness by supporting you with its gentle and loving vibrations. You could also turn to Black Moonstone, Rhodochrosite or Pink Tourmaline.

WISDOM
AND FREEDOM

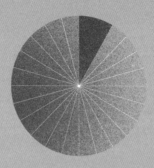

Sagittarius season is represented by the archer who shoots high and blazes a trail into new territory. The archer is also a centaur – half horse and half human, half wild and half philosophical. Sagittarius season is a time to feel fiercely alive and simultaneously inspired to ask big, existential questions. It's a season for expanding your boundaries and traveling physically and mentally to understand more about the world and the human experience.

TAURUS HOROSCOPE
FOR SAGITTARIUS SEASON

Dance with themes of trust, forgiveness and letting go. These are all emotional topics. By sitting with your feelings, you can discover deep mindset patterns, heal and grow. Through self-reflection and emotional processing, you may discover situations in which you would like to forgive others and move on. Let go to make room for new beginnings.

Morning Practice

Go for a walk or
a jog out in nature.

Evening Practice

Memorize an
inspiring quote.

CRYSTALS FOR
SAGITTARIUS SEASON

INNER WISDOM

Azurite   In Sagittarius season, the archer knows that the best
way to take aim is to trust your inner wisdom. When you are
connected to your true self, it's easier to make choices. Life
feels more satisfying. Azurite is the stone to hold and carry
when you want to bolster your self-confidence and tune into
your wisdom. Or choose Idocrase, Shattuckite or Amethyst.

EXPANSION

Jasper   Ruled by the gas giant Jupiter, Sagittarius is the
sign of expansion. During this season, you can move beyond
anything that is limiting you. Is there an area of your life in
which you feel trapped in a cage? Maybe if you take a closer
look, you'll find that the door to the cage has been open the
entire time. Feel the freedom and expansion that is available
to you with the help of Jasper. This enlivening stone will help
you break out into new territory. Alternatives are Blue Topaz,
Pink Chalcedony or Ruby Iolite.

ADVENTURE AND TRAVEL

Turquoise   When you're setting out in search of new
horizons, reach for Turquoise as your talisman for protection
and luck. Travel and adventure require equal parts bravery
and boldness, but the reward is an expanded mindset and
perspective. Let Turquoise be your steady support system as
you push beyond your boundaries to discover excitement,
new opportunity and enlightenment. You could also use
Green Opal, Smoky Quartz or Aventurine.

CAREER
AND GOALS

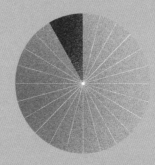

Like the mountain goat, in Capricorn season
you are primed to choose your footing carefully as
you make your ascent. Capricorn season brings practical
and productive forward motion. Use this energy efficiently
and tactically. You may choose to counterbalance this drive
and ambition with a large dose of acceptance, both
of yourself and others. Remember to give yourself a
break; you are trying your best.

TAURUS HOROSCOPE
FOR CAPRICORN SEASON

What do you value most? Your values can point you in the direction of inspiration. Your values spark your goals. You'll know you've identified one of your core values when you feel fired up and excited. The Sun is currently touring your sector of philosophy and expansion. Connect with what you believe in and let that inform your growth.

Morning Practice

Write down your goals.

Evening Practice

Reflect on your
accomplishments.

CRYSTALS FOR CAPRICORN SEASON

ACHIEVEMENT

Fluorite   Your Capricorn season recommendation supports
you in taking things one step at a time while staying focused
on your big picture goals. Look to Fluorite. Fluorite's unique
vibration can help you concentrate, while energizing you so
that you can keep moving forwards. Or look for support from
Ocean Jasper, Septarian Nodule or Tiger's Eye.

CAREER

Cat's Eye   Capricorn season is a wonderful time to take
stock. While you think about your work life, keep Cat's Eye by
your side. This stone helps you know your strengths, which is
imperative for a fulfilling career. It will help you feel optimistic
and believe in yourself. Cat's Eye's structured energy helps
you know your personal boundaries and make smart money
choices. You could also use Andradite Garnet, Apatite or
Hawk's Eye.

FOR SELF-ACCEPTANCE

Blue Aragonite   Let calming Blue Aragonite guide you
when you need to feel the soothing balm of self-acceptance.
Capricorn season pushes you to achieve, which may cause
you to question your progress in life. Counterbalance that by
learning to accept yourself for who you are. Blue Aragonite
has a compassionate energy that may inspire you to be less
judgemental towards yourself and show yourself more kindness.
Other crystals for self-acceptance are Prasiolite, Amethyst
or Shungite.

FRIENDSHIP AND VISION

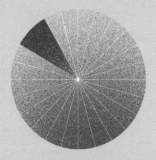

Aquarius season pushes people and ideas to the forefront. What are your big ideas for the future? And who is in your community? Your vision for the future may also be a vision for humanity. Take the time to research causes to which you might contribute time, money and resources. Your friends, communities and social groups are extra important during this season, so prioritize the people who mean the most to you.

TAURUS HOROSCOPE FOR AQUARIUS SEASON

With the Sun lighting up your area of achievement, goals and career, focus on your ambitions. Dream big, then do a little planning to set new goals that are aligned with your visions. You may feel like working harder than usual. Be systematic as you build the functional structures that support your dreams.

Morning Practice

reate a vision board and make it the
·st thing you see when you wake up.

Evening Practice

Call a friend for a
meaningful chat.

FRIENDSHIP

Bismuth   Aquarius season asks you to turn towards your
community. What can you offer? What will you receive?
Friends enrich your life in so many ways, but mostly by
encouraging your feeling of belonging – a natural mood
booster. Bismuth has an expansive energy that helps you join
with others in a shared sense of community. Carry Bismuth as a
reminder that you are connected to others. Or you could reach
for Carnelian, Sunset Sodalite or Blue Apatite.

FAITH IN THE FUTURE

Cavansite   The future is uncertain. Sometimes you need a
boost to help you trust in the potential and possibility of what
the future can become. In that case, reach for Cavansite.
This stone has a sweet vibe of positivity that can give you the
courage to believe in your biggest dreams for the future. Some
alternatives are Peridot, Muscovite or Auralite 23.

VIBRATIONAL LIFT

Apophyllite   When Aquarius season asks you to turn
your attention to what is possible, it helps to have a positive
outlook. Without suppressing any challenging feelings (those
are important and need to be processed), pay some special
attention to the positive things in your life and work to create
an enduring, positive mindset. If you need a little extra support,
reach for Clear or Green Apophyllite. This high-vibe crystal
can lift your spirits and help you feel full of potential. You
could also try Quartz, Hematite or Angelite.

INTUITION AND SPIRITUALITY

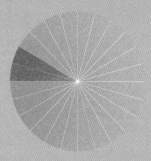

The most mystical season of all, Pisces season is the time to tune into your intuition. Slide like a slippery fish into the sphere of your dreams, faith, spirituality, compassion and creativity. This is a moment to rest, reflect and look inwards. Reconnect with your imagination. Feel your feelings. Plug into your spirituality or whatever makes you feel connected to the universe.

TAURUS HOROSCOPE FOR PISCES SEASON

Turn your attention towards the future. The Sun is moving through your chart in the area of community and future visions. If you were to let go of realistic or practical considerations, if anything were possible, what would you imagine for your life and for society as a whole? This process of envisioning can be uplifting.

Morning Practice

Record your dreams.

Evening Practice

Do some freewriting
to clear your mind.

COMPASSION

Lavender Quartz   Lavender Quartz helps you feel peace and
understanding for others. It will bestow upon you the softness
that you need to open up to other people's perspectives. It will
also allow you to dissolve drama with a heightened sense of
empathy. This soothing and healing stone can offer strength
while you stand in someone else's shoes. A compassionate life
is a fulfilling life. As an alternative, turn to Thulite, Prehnite
with Epidote or Fluorite.

INTUITION

Pink Opal   When you trust your inner guidance system you
have ultimate clarity. Harness the power of your intuition
in Pisces season with the help of Pink Opal. This stone will
help you connect to yourself and to your guides. It raises
the volume on your inner 'Yes' or 'No' by quietening any
distractions and helping you connect within. Other crystals
for intuition are Clear Quartz, Moldavite or Dumortierite.

FOR FAITH

Celestite   Faith can be thought of as a complete trust or
confidence in someone or something. With a little bit of
faith you may find it easier to contend with fear or anxiety.
But trust and faith must be developed from within. In Pisces
season, harness the power of high-vibrational Celestite to
help you move beyond unnecessary fears as you put your
trust in something bigger. You could also use Vatican Stone,
Apophyllite or Turquoise.

LUNAR ENERGY AND MERCURY IN MOTION

THE LUNAR
CYCLE

In astrology, the Moon is a catalyst, helping us to move forwards with our goals and intentions.

The 29-day lunar cycle begins in darkness. The Moon then appears as a faint crescent and grows bigger until it's full. This process, from darkness to Full Moon, mirrors the incubation and development of your own creative process. Then, the Moon wanes until it completely disappears, reflecting another stage of the creative cycle – the process of releasing your efforts and making space for another cycle to begin. This allows new thoughts and ideas to emerge.

Each of the eight phases of the Moon cycle offers a different type of energy, which we will explore in this chapter. You can follow the Moon through the lunar month with crystal recommendations, setting your intentions in alignment with the New Moon and letting the lunar cycle help you make that intention into reality. The lunar cycle will also help you cleanse and release so that you can gently transition into the next phase.

By using crystals to work with the lunar cycle you can activate the potential of the Moon and amplify its energy. Through visualization or meditation, tap into the unique energies of each stage of the Moon cycle with the following crystals. For the suggested rituals at each phase, choose a crystal from the recommended options, or substitute with your favourite crystal.

Sun

New Moon

Waxing Crescent

Waning Crescent

First Quarter

Earth

Third Quarter

Waxing Gibbous

Waning Gibbous

Full Moon

SET YOUR NEW INTENTIONS

The Moon is dark. This is a time for reflection and a time to connect with your inner self. Use your energy to envision what you would like to make happen. What do you desire? What are your dreams? Anything is possible – imagine that you are planting seeds of intention that will manifest and grow throughout the Waxing Moon Phase. The New Moon is a quiet and emotional time and you may discover that, as you think about what you would like to create, many different feelings arise. Excitement, anticipation, fear, worry – whatever feelings arise, make space for those feelings and be gentle with yourself. Listen to your intuition and imagine your next steps.

Black Moonstone can support you during the delicate and sensitive New Moon vibration. It offers wellsprings of patience and peace as you work with your emotions and reflect on your life. When your dreams are germinating under the surface, Black Moonstone can help you trust your own process.

Labradorite opens your third eye wide so that you can tune into your intuition, and design your goals in accordance with your path and purpose.

Pink Sapphire's loving energy can buffer you and help you feel emotionally at ease.

Ametrine provides sweet joy and concentrated focus so that you can set intentions with confidence.

TRUST,
INSPIRATION, SERENITY
AND DELIGHT

New Moon Ritual

Freewrite about what you yearn for and anything else that's on your mind. Then jot down your intentions for this Moon cycle on a piece of paper and place your chosen crystal on top.

NURTURE YOUR INTENTIONS

Your seeds of intention are germinating under the soil, and maybe some of the plants are just beginning to sprout. As the lunar energy builds momentum, make sure that you have the resources you need to achieve your goals. Provide structure and support for yourself. This cycle is just beginning to take shape, so consider how your choices will determine your direction – maybe there are changes you'd like to make to your goals. Remain curious throughout this process, because anything is possible!

Turquoise is a powerhouse of a crystal that can deftly carry you through the precarious Waxing Crescent phase. At this moment you need a subtle combination of confidence, discernment, curiosity and commitment. Turquoise can help you understand the truth of what you need to create, and it can help you stay open and accepting of your process. Use this stone as you decide what you really want to manifest and commit to during this Moon cycle.

Shattuckite helps you intuitively illuminate your path so that you can make the decisions that are right for you.

Pyrite offers crystalline protection and is a wonderful choice to help you realize your goals.

Orange Calcite gives you mental focus and lots of energy for the journey ahead.

TRUTH,
INTUITION, MANIFESTATION
AND FOCUS

Waxing Crescent Moon Ritual

Read and rewrite your intentions for this Moon cycle.
Decorate the paper and place your chosen crystal back on top.

BUILD YOUR MOMENTUM

Look around your garden of intentions and discover what is growing. Have your goals started to take shape? If so, how are they coming along? Do you need more support? Perhaps you have had surprising results? At the First Quarter Moon the constraints of reality can be intimidating. You have big dreams, but sometimes you encounter resistance when dreams make contact with real world limitations. Maybe there is more work required than you had foreseen, or there are real-world issues with time, money, support or other resources. Give yourself lots of encouragement. Pivot, and reassess if necessary. This is an exciting, high energy time, so keep taking action and building momentum.

Bumblebee Jasper When reality, and all of its limitations, hits, Bumblebee Jasper can help you stay the course with confidence. Lean on this crystal when you need the energy to just keep moving forwards. It will subdue your fears and inspire you to push past your comfort zone.

Peridot is a cheery companion that will help you look at any situation with optimism.

Tangerine Quartz offers creative potential that makes problem solving effortless.

Aventurine will vitalize you and give you the confidence to keep going.

CONFIDENCE,
OPTIMISM, CREATIVITY AND
VITALITY

First Quarter Moon Ritual

Light a candle, hold your chosen crystal and visualize your intentions being realized.

DEVELOP YOUR INTENTIONS

It's astonishing what a little effort can create! Now that you've made it to the Waxing Gibbous phase of the Moon cycle, you are starting to see the effects of the intentions that you set. If your goal was to improve your nutrition, you may be feeling better already. If you felt motivated to get out there and start dating, you may have started some new conversations. Whatever the last few days have revealed, now is the time to roll up your sleeves and actively give shape to your garden. What will you weed out? What is working, and what isn't working? What changes might you make? The intensity has almost peaked to take tender care of your emotional well-being as you keep putting in effort towards your dreams.

Jet Jet's grounding energy will help you establish deep root systems for your developing intentions. When you need strength and motivation to keep pushing forwards with your goals, this stone will support you. As a bonus, jet has a sheltering vibration that can steady you emotionally and help you surge forwards with optimism and hope.

Hematite offers balance and protection, helping you proactively take care of yourself during this active time.

Carnelian lights your fire with sparkling enthusiasm and convinces you to tune into your creative side.

Blue Lace Agate calms your mind, allowing you to weed through your options and make solid decisions.

GROUNDING,
PROTECTION, ENTHUSIASM
AND PEACE OF MIND

Waxing Gibbous Moon Ritual

While holding or wearing your chosen crystal, do something that feels active or expressive, such as dancing, painting, gardening, cooking or singing. Imagine your goals and repeat your intentions.

HARVEST

Everything is revealed under the light of the Moon. The attempts you've made, your wins, your losses. It's time to get out in the garden and harvest the crop. Regardless of whether the bounty lives up to your expectations, there is something to appreciate and celebrate. At the Full Moon, honour what you've created and give gratitude to yourself for your commitment. This phase represents the push and pull of two opposite energies as the Moon is in the opposite sign to the Sun. The result is a highly polarized and intense energy that can heighten emotions, pull you in two different directions, or cause you to realize something important. Make sure to be very gentle with yourself and those around you.

EMOTIONAL EXPLORATION, ABUNDANCE, PEACEFULNESS AND RECEPTIVITY

White Moonstone symbolizes the Full Moon and all of its glorious creativity and excitement. This pearly white crystal shines a bright light so that you can see clearly. As you examine the fruits that you've cultivated during the Waxing Moon phase, use the receptive and healing energy of White Moonstone to help you accept and celebrate. It's time for gratitude, and this comforting crystal will help you open up to that feeling.

Green Apatite is an antidote to the drama of the Full Moon – use it to highlight joy and abundance.

Jade has a subtle, soothing energy that imparts an optimistic attitude.

Stilbite connects the heart, mind and intuition – this can help you rationally balance your emotions while still opening up to divine insight.

Full Moon Ritual

Hold your chosen crystal and write down three things that you are grateful for. The Full Moon is also a great time to cleanse your crystals. Place them outside or on a windowsill and let them bathe in the Moon's healing energy.

REFLECT AND REVIEW

Now that the intensity of the full reveal has begun to wane, you can settle deeper into your new reality. Indulge yourself and enjoy. As the Moon has moved through waxing to waning, this is the beginning of a less active and more receptive phase. This means that you can simply sit with the ebbing fullness of what is. Begin a process of compassionate review. What have you learned? What will you do differently in the next Moon cycle? Each lunar cycle reveals an older, more experienced version of who you are becoming. So sink into this moment of reflection and get to know yourself once more.

Obsidian offers a protective energy that buffers and supports. Use it at the Waning Gibbous phase of the Moon cycle to release the past and securely recline into the experience of the moment. Obsidian's cleansing vibes can help you remove any junk from your thought patterns, allowing you to think from a new perspective. Harness its clarifying energy to appraise your situation with equanimity and objectivity.

Tiger's Eye is for encouragement and strength as you review your progress and make plans for improvement.

Citrine offers joy and optimism so that you can look at your accomplishments through a positive lens.

Celestite provides tranquillity as you come down off the high of the Full Moon.

PROTECTION, STRENGTH, JOY AND TRANQUILLITY

Waning Gibbous Moon Ritual

Pour yourself some tea, water, or other drink of your choice, and take the time to sit and quietly appreciate the moment. With your chosen crystal nearby, review your intention and gratitude lists.

LET GO

Get comfortable letting go so that you can make space for new things. At the Last Quarter Moon allow the leaves to fall and the fading plants to return to the soil. A tree drops its leaves to conserve resources. Take stock of what you want to let go of, so that you can use your energy wisely. Is there someone you need to forgive? Do you need to release your expectations and accept something about your life? Release the past or an outdated way of thinking, let go and forgive. Maybe you declutter your closet, acknowledge your reality, admit your mistakes, get really honest with yourself, or forgive yourself or others. The Last Quarter Moon asks that you put in a little effort to let go of the emotions and ideas that are taking up excess energy.

LOVE, SUPPORT, GROUNDING AND GENTLE SELF-REFLECTION

Rose Quartz is an emotional balm that can help you forgive yourself and others. As the Last Quarter Moon inspires you to release your expectations and accept your current reality, you need a soothing support that helps you open up compassionately. Rose Quartz brings playful, loving vibes and helps you gently accept a situation and move forwards.

Rutilated Quartz offers a powerful support in following through on your intentions as you review what you've learned and plan for the next phase.

Smoky Quartz provides grounding, protection and assistance in clearing the thoughts and feelings that you are ready to release.

Amethyst is for gently releasing old mental patterns and contemplating new possibilities.

Last Quarter Moon Ritual

Create a peaceful environment and run a bath for yourself. Place a water-safe, non-toxic crystal (such as Quartz or Amethyst) in the bath while you review your intentions from this moon cycle. Repeat these affirmations, 'I make space for clarity' and 'I release the past'.

STILLNESS AND REST

The lunar energy is encouraging you to turn inwards and be still. All is quiet in the winter of your metaphorical garden. Embracing stillness offers many benefits. By allowing your inner landscape to exist without judgement, you honour who you are now. Slowing down can also help you uncover your values and emotional truth – which may not be so apparent when you are busily running around. And last but not least, rest and quiet will help you recharge your energy for the next cycle. Challenge yourself to slow down and be present in the moment. There will be ample time for new plans and dreams when the next cycle begins.

CONNECTION WITH NATURE, CLEANSING, SOOTHING AND REFLECTION

Serpentine can help you open a gateway to the stillness within and to the profound interconnectedness of the universe. Using this crystal during your Waning Crescent Moon meditations will help you feel buffered and supported in the understanding that there is no-one you need to be and nothing you need to do. Float along with the waves of existence. You'll know when the time is right again for action.

Selenite radiates cleansing energy that can help you release the past cycle and prepare to make a fresh start.

Howlite soothes your spirit and quietens any absurd complaints from your 'inner critic'.

Aquamarine helps you create a meditative state of mind so that you can listen to the stillness within.

Waning Crescent Moon Ritual

Sit quietly in the meditation of your choosing. Hold your crystal or place it nearby.

MERCURY
RETROGRADE

Mercury Retrograde deserves attention as it's a chance to review your plans and goals. It's notoriously known for causing technology and communication issues, but the upside of this time period is that it offers an invitation to slow down and re-assess where you are and where you want to go.

Fast-moving Mercury symbolizes connection, communication and technology. Mercury is the part of you that learns, thinks, teaches and talks.

Mercury orbits the Sun about four times as fast as the Earth and every time that Mercury zips past the Earth an optical illusion occurs that makes it look as though Mercury is moving backwards. When Mercury appears to be moving backwards (Mercury Retrograde), it's a great opportunity to slow down. Go back over your thoughts and decisions of recent months and review them. Turn inwards to gain guidance from your intuition.

Mercury Retrograde happens about three times a year and lasts for about three weeks each time. You can use these retrograde periods as a moment to check in with yourself and review your practices, thoughts and relationships. Have you been putting off an uncomfortable conversation? Is there something that you need to be honest about with yourself when it comes to relationships, work or money? What has your body been trying to tell you? Is there some new way that you could step out of your comfort zone? What would help you feel more secure and supported?

Underlying issues tend to rise to the surface during Mercury Retrograde. It's typically advised to make sure that you are extra clear in your communications during these periods, and that you wait until the retrograde period has ended before beginning new projects or signing contracts. But it's an excellent time to pick up where you left off on something – to rethink, redo and review.

YOUR CRYSTAL PRACTICE DURING MERCURY RETROGRADE

Crystal energy can help you slow down your busy mind and tune into your intuition during Mercury Retrograde. As you rethink and review, these crystals will amplify your intuition and clarity.

KEEN INSIGHT

Pietersite   Employ this speckled Quartz for illuminated insight paired with steady determination.

CLARITY AND COMMUNICATION

Aquamarine   This stone soothes and calms the mind while simultaneously boosting your ability to communicate clearly.

CREATIVE THOUGHT

Citrine   A crystal that spurs your imagination, helping you conceptualize how you might like patterns or situations to change.

Beginning of Mercury Retrograde Ritual

Perform a full and gentle review of the issues most affecting you by writing a journal entry using the following prompt: 'What do I need to see that I'm not seeing when it comes to my …' Give yourself lots of gratitude in the process and call on your chosen crystal to provide understanding and clarity. When you've finished, write down three takeaways on a small piece of paper and place your crystal on top of it for the remainder of the Retrograde. Drawing on the power of your crystal, let your subconscious mind continue to explore and reveal the subtleties of these thoughts and questions over the coming weeks.

End of Mercury Retrograde Ritual

Near the end of the Retrograde cycle, set an intention to integrate what you've learned during the past days and weeks. Begin by returning to your piece of paper and your crystal. What came up for you during Mercury Retrograde? Was there a new realization, attitude or interest that emerged? Think about what you may have realized and journal about what you'd like to bring into your life now. Is there an intention (see page 22) or affirmation that could come from this exploration? If so, write it down. Look in a mirror and repeat your intention or affirmation five times while holding your crystal. Remember to thank your crystal and to thank yourself for showing up. For the next two weeks, repeat this daily ritual.

CONCLUSION

This book has taken you deep below the Earth's surface, through the metaphorical caverns of crystals and their symbolism. You've connected the dots of the solar system and the meaning of the astrology you were born with. By pairing the forces of the stars above with the crystals below, you've gained tools that can help you navigate your unique journey with wisdom.

In Part Two, you learned about the crystals that can support your unique astrology. This section included insights for Taurus Sun, Moon and Rising signs, along with supportive crystal recommendations for what your sign needs in five key life areas.

Life is always changing and so in Part Three you learned to follow the energy of the Sun as it moves on its annual journey through the zodiac, finding crystals that may help you elaborate on the theme of each astrological season.

Revolving and evolving with changing astrological cycles continued in Part Four, where you paired crystal energy with the ebb and flow of the Moon, and learned to harness the power of crystals in tandem with Mercury Retrograde to perform a trimonthly check-in.

All the answers are already within you. When you choose a crystal, you awaken the vibration of that crystal within yourself. Harness your astro-crystal practice to help you see what already exists inside of you. You have everything you need.

With the cosmos above and the crystals below, you are always connected and supported. Let the stones and the stars strengthen your self-awareness and self-trust as you continue your crystalline cosmic journey.

Crystals and astrology are not intended to be a substitute for medical advice, diagnosis or treatment. Always seek the advice of your qualified healthcare provider.

RESOURCES

GET YOUR BIRTH CHART	www.sandysitron.com/crystals
ASTROLOGY READING	www.sandysitron.com
CRYSTALS	**101 Power Crystals:** *The Ultimate Guide to Magical Crystals, Gems, and Stones for Healing and Transformation* Judy Hall
CRYSTAL ENERGY HEALING	https://www.kalisaaugustine.com/
SOURCING CRYSTALS RESPONSIBLY	moonrisecrystals.com/
SPIRAL CRYSTALS	spiralcrystals.com/
HOOF AND PAW	hoofandpawuk.com/
ASTROLOGY	**Astrology for Yourself** Demetra George and Douglas Bloch
AFFIRMATION WORK	Transformational coach Dana Balicki: https://danabalicki.com/
AFFIRMATION WORK	**Empowerment:** *The Art of Creating Your Life as You Want It* Gail Straub and David Gershon
ASTROLOGY EDUCATION	www.thestrology.com
	Ritual Enchantments *A Modern Witch's Guide to Self-Possession* Mya Spalter

FEATURED CRYSTALS

LAURENCE KING

First published in Great Britain in 2022 by Laurence King
an imprint of The Orion Publishing Group Ltd
Carmelite House, 50 Victoria Embankment
London EC4Y 0DZ

An Hachette UK Company

10 9 8 7 6 5 4 3 2 1

A CIP catalogue record for this book is
available from the British Library.

ISBN 978-0-8578-2932-0

Design: Therese Vandling

Printed in China by C&C Offset Printing Co. Ltd

Laurence King Publishing is committed to ethical and
sustainable production. We are proud participants in the
Book Chain Project®. [bookchainproject.com]

**BOOK
CHAIN
PROJECT**

www.laurenceking.com
www.orionbooks.co.uk